MW01515868

Lives of the Saints

Our Lady of Fatima

with Prayers and Devotions

Edited by
Mark Etling

RP

**Regina
Press**

Nihil Obstat: Reverend Robert O. Morrissey, J.C.D.
                       Censor librorum
                       November 18, 2004

Imprimatur: Most Reverend William Murphy
                       Bishop of Rockville Centre
                       November 21, 2004

THE REGINA PRESS
10 Hub Drive
Melville, New York 11747

Florentine Collection™, All rights reserved worldwide.
Imported exclusively by Malco.

Printed in U.S.A.

ISBN : 0-88271-763-4

Introduction

*T*he apparitions at Fatima occurred during a time of international strife and unrest. The brutal First World War had been dragging on for almost three years, with no end in sight. The centuries-old reign of the czars was coming to a violent close with the onset of the Russian Revolution.

In the midst of all this suffering and inhumanity the Virgin Mary appeared to three young peasant children at Fatima in Portugal. She spoke to the children of Fatima, and to the world, about the need for conversion, to turn away from the sins of violence and injustice and to return to the God of mercy and love. She spoke of the need for peace, and asked that all the people of the world pray for peace.

The world we live in today is filled with tension and unrest, just as it was when our Lady of Fatima appeared. It seems that every day we hear about the horrors of war, terrorism, and religious conflict. And the world's violence seems only to beget even more violence.

At this time in history, just as in 1917, there is a deep and profound need for conversion. There is a need for conversion of minds and hearts from injustice to justice, form violence to peace, from hatred to love. There is a crying need for conversion among nations, in communities, within families, and in ourselves.

Our Lady of Fatima can be the inspiration for greater conversion today, just as she was in 1917. And she remains, now and always, our Queen of Peace.

The Story of
Our Lady of Fatima

*B*elievers often say that God works in mysterious ways. God frequently seems to choose the most humble and least expected of his people to reveal himself and his holy will for humanity. This was surely the case with the children of Fatima.

Lucia dos Santos and her two younger cousins, Francisco and Jacinta Marto, were poor shepherd children from the obscure village of Aljustrel in the Fatima region of Portugal. Although their families were devout Christians, they had done nothing to distinguish themselves in the eyes of the world.

But on May 13, 1917, the lives of Lucia, Francisco and Jacinta were forever changed. On that beautiful Sunday afternoon the three were together at the Covia da Iria, two miles west of Fatima. Suddenly a brilliant flash of lightning drew their attention. Then a beautiful Lady in shining white robes appeared to them. She spoke to them, asking them to return to that same spot on the thirteenth day of each month at the same time for the next six months.

Each time the children returned faithfully to the site, and each time the Lady reappeared, just as she had promised. She told them that she had been sent by God with a message for every person who would live in the twentieth century. She asked the children to pray the rosary daily for the conversion of sinners, and for peace in the world.

She also asked for increased devotion to her Immaculate Heart. She spoke of the need for prayer and acts of penance for the conversion of Russia, which in 1917 was experiencing the violent Communist revolution. She also encouraged the observance of the first Saturdays of each month by celebrating the Sacrament of Reconciliation and receiving the Holy Eucharist.

At the heart of the Lady's message to the world were three "secrets" which she revealed to the children during her appearance in July. The first secret was a vision of hell, which was said to refer to the two world wars. This vision was accompanied by an urgent plea from the

Lady for prayer and sacrifices. The second secret contained the Lady's solemn request for the consecration of Russia, and her prediction that Russia would one day return to Christianity. The third secret would remain known only to the Pope and certain Vatican officials until the year 2000. In it the Lady spoke of the failed assassination attempt against Pope John Paul II in 1981.

The apparitions gained such notoriety that on October 13, a crowd of some 70,000 from all over Portugal gathered in a rainstorm to witness the Lady's final appearance. On that day she finally identified herself as "Our Lady of the Rosary." Then the children saw three tableaus: first, the Holy Family with St. Joseph and the Christ Child; second, Our Lady of Sorrows with her grieving Son; and third, Our Lady of Mt. Carmel holding the Infant Jesus.

The crowd saw none of this, but instead witnessed an incredible sight. As they looked on the storm dissipated, and the sun became like a silver disk, and then seemed to dance in the sky. It began to whirl and then stopped, and then it began to spin again, and even appeared to plunge toward the crowd. Finally it resumed its natural position. This spectacle came to be known as the "Miracle of the Sun."

The apparitions to the children of Fatima have been commemorated by believers ever since. Soon after the last appearance a small archway was built at the site, followed by a tiny chapel. When the chapel was destroyed by dynamite in 1922, a second chapel was built near it. Then on October 13, 1928 the foundation stone for the Basilica of Our Lady of the Rosary was laid. The basilica would not be completed and dedicated until 1953.

In 1930, after a lengthy inquiry, the bishop of the diocese of Leiria, in which Fatima is located, approved the devotion to Our Lady of Fatima. By 1942, devotion to Our Lady of Fatima had grown so much that Pope Pius XII consecrated the entire world to the Immaculate Heart of Mary in honor of the twenty-fifth anniversary of the apparitions.

On May 13, 1982, Pope John Paul II celebrated the Eucharist in Fatima on the first anniversary of the attempt on his life. He gave thanks for Mary's intercession in sparing his life. On that occasion he reconsecrated the world to Mary's Immaculate Heart and called the world to prayer.

Sadly, two of the three children of Fatima did not receive the blessing of long life. Francisco Marto died on April 4, 1919, and Jacinta passed away on February 20, 1920. During his Fatima visit in 2000, Pope John Paul II beatified Francisco and Jacinta. Sister Lucia, a member of the Carmelites, lived to be 97 years old. She died on February 13, 2005.

Prayers to Our Lady of Fatima

Litany to Our Lady of Fatima

*O*ur Lady of Fatima,
   pray for our beloved country.
Our Lady of Fatima,
   sanctify our clergy.
Our Lady of Fatima,
   make our Catholics more fervent.
Our Lady of Fatima,
   guide and inspire those who govern us.
Our Lady of Fatima,
   cure the sick who confide in you.
Our Lady of Fatima,
   console the sorrowfulwho trust in you.
Our Lady of Fatima,
   help those who invokeyour aid.
Our Lady of Fatima,
   deliver us from all dangers.
Our Lady of Fatima,
   help us to resist temptation.
Our Lady of Fatima,
   obtain for us all that we lovingly ask of you.
Our Lady of Fatima,
   help those who are dear to us.

Our Lady of Fatima,
 bring to the Church all persons of good will.
Our Lady of Fatima,
 increase our devotion to Christ.
Our Lady of Fatima,
 obtain for us the pardon of our sins.
Our Lady of Fatima,
 bring all humanity to the feet
  of your divine Son.
Our Lady of Fatima,
 obtain peace for the world.
O Mary conceived without sin,
 pray for us who have recourse to you.
Immaculate Heart of Mary,
 pray for us now
  and at the hour of our death.
 Amen.

Let us pray: O God of infinite mercy and goodness, fill our hearts with a great confidence in your dear Mother, whom we invoke under the title of Our Lady of the Rosary and Our Lady of Fatima, and grant us by her powerful intercession all the blessings, spiritual and temporal, that we need. Through Christ our Lord. Amen.

Act of Consecration to the Immaculate Heart of Mary

O Immaculate Heart of Mary, queen of heaven and earth, and tender mother of us all, in accordance with your wishes made known at Fatima, I consecrate to your Immaculate Heart myself, my brothers and sisters, my country and the whole human race.

Reign over us, most holy Mother of God, and teach us how to make the heart of your Son, our Lord Jesus Christ, reign and triumph in us even as it has reigned and triumphed in you.

Reign over us, most Blessed Virgin, that we may be yours in prosperity and in adversity, in joy and in sorrow, in health and in sickness, in life and in death.

O most compassionate Heart of Mary, Queen of heaven, watch over our minds and hearts and preserve them from the impurity which you lamented so sorrowfully at Fatima. Assist us in imitating you in all things, especially purity. Help us to call down upon our country and upon the whole world the peace of God in justice and charity.

Therefore, most gracious Virgin and Mother, I

hereby promise to imitate your virtues by the practice of a truly Christian life.

I resolve to receive the Holy Eucharist regularly and to offer to you five decades of the rosary each day, together with my sacrifices, in the spirit of reparation and reconciliation. Amen.

The Sub Tuum

O most blessed Virgin Mary, Mother of Jesus Christ and Mother of the Church, open our hearts to the great anticipation for the proclamation of the Gospel to the whole of creation and the reign of God. Your Mother is ever mindful of the many dangers and evils which threaten to overpower men and women in our time. O Mary, full of courage, may your spiritual strength and trust in God inspire us, so that we might know how to overcome the obstacles that we encounter. Teach us to treat the affairs of the world with a real sense of Christian responsibility and a joyful hope for the coming of God's reign.

O Mother of our divine Savior and our Mother, who gathered with the apostles in prayer at the Cenacle, awaiting the coming of the Holy Spirit at Pentecost, we implore you for a renewed outpouring of the Spirit upon all the faithful so that we, your children, might more generously respond to the will of your divine Son and the mission of his Church. O virgin Mother, guide and sustain us so that we might always live as true sons and daughters of the Church of your Son Jesus Christ. Enable us to do our part in helping to establish here on earth a civilization of truth and love, as God will it, and for his greater glory. Amen.

Prayer to Our Lady of Fatima for Peace

O Mary, Mother of God and Queen of Peace, you appeared to the children of Fatima at a time of great unrest and turmoil in the world. You asked then that the world pray for peace, so that the Reign of God may be known in every land.

Our world today continues to be mired in the vicious and fruitless cycle of hatred, violence and war. Your message of peace to the children of Fatima is needed as urgently today as it was when you first delivered it.

Grant us, Mary, that peace which is so much more than the mere absence of war. Grant us God's peace, so that we might see every man and woman as a brother or a sister, as fellow creatures of the one God. Help us to build a world of justice, which is the only sure foundation of peace. And bring us all one day into the fulness of union with the Father, Son and Holy Spirit in eternity. This we ask through Christ, your Son and our Lord, the Prince of Peace. Amen.

Prayer to Our Lady of Fatima for the Children of the World

O Mary, you freely and lovingly embraced the will of God for you by accepting the call to be the Mother of his Son. With the help of St. Joseph you raised the child Jesus so that he grew in wisdom, age and grace before God and humanity.

You appeared to the children of Fatima, confiding in them, though they be young and unknown, to reveal to the world your message of conversion and peace.

We ask you now, Our Lady of Fatima, to gather all the children of the world into your loving embrace. Grant them God's gifts of health and peace, of security and love. Help them to know and use the many gifts and talents they have been given for the betterment of the one human race. Inspire them one day to be men and women of peace.

O Lord, through the intercession of your Mother Mary, bless and keep your children. Amen.

Prayer of Cardinal Newman

O Mother of Jesus and my mother, let me dwell with you, cling to you and love you with ever-increasing love. I promise the honor, love and trust of a child. Give me a mother's protection, for I need your watchful care. You know better than any other the thoughts and desires of the Sacred Heart. Keep constantly before my mind the same thoughts, the same desires, that my heart may be filled with zeal for the interests of the Sacred Heart of your divine Son. Instill in me a love of all that is noble, that I may no longer be easily turned to selfishness.

Help me, dearest mother, to acquire the virtues that God wants of me: to forget myself always, to work solely for him, without fear of sacrifice. I shall always rely on your help to be what Jesus wants me to be. I am his; I am yours, my good mother! Give me each day your holy and maternal blessing until my last evening on earth, when your Immaculate Heart will present me to the heart of Jesus in heaven, there to love and bless you and your divine Son for all eternity.

Marian Prayer of Pope John Paul II:
"Mother of All Men and Women and of All Peoples"

*H*ail to you, who are wholly united to the redeeming consecration of your Son!

Mother of the Church! Enlighten the People of God along the paths of faith, hope and love! Enlighten especially the peoples whose consecration and entrustment by us you are awaiting. Help us to live in the truth of the consecration of Christ for the entire human family of the modern world.

In entrusting to you, O Mother, the world, all individuals and peoples, we also entrust to you this very consecration of the world, placing it in your motherly heart.

Immaculate Heart! Help us to conquer the menace of evil, which so easily takes root in the hearts of the people of today, and whose immeasurable effects already weigh down upon our modern world and seem to block the paths towards the future.

From famine and war, deliver us. From nuclear war, from incalculable self-destruction, from every kind of war, deliver us. From sins against the life of humanity from its very beginning, deliver us.

From hatred and from the demeaning of the dignity of the children of God, deliver us.

From every kind of injustice in the life of society, both national and international, deliver us. From readiness to trample on the commandments of God, deliver us.

From attempts to stifle in human hearts the very truth of God, deliver us.

From the loss of awareness of good and evil, deliver us. From sins against the Holy Spirit, deliver us.

Accept, O Mother of Christ, this cry laden with the sufferings of all individual human beings, laden with the sufferings of whole societies.

Help us with the power of the Holy Spirit to conquer all sin: individual sin and the "sin of the world," sin in all its manifestations.

Let there be revealed, once more, in the history of the world the infinite saving power of the Redemption: the power of merciful love! May it put a stop to evil! May it transform consciences! May your Immaculate Heart reveal for all the light of hope!

Marian Prayer of Pope John Paul II:
"O Mary Bright Dawn of the New World"

O Mary, bright dawn of the new world, Mother of the living, to you do we entrust the cause of life:

Look down, O Mother, Upon the vast numbers of babies not allowed to be born, of the poor whose lives are made difficult, of men and women who are victims of brutal violence, of the elderly and the sick killed by indifference or out of misguided mercy. Grant that all who believe in your Son may proclaim the Gospel of life with honesty and love to the people of our time.

Obtain for them the grace to accept that Gospel as a gift ever new, the joy of celebrating it with gratitude throughout their lives and the courage to bear witness to it resolutely, in order to build, together with all people of good will, the civilization of truth and love, to the praise and glory of God, the Creator and lover of life.

Daily Marian Prayers of Pope John Paul II

Sunday

*M*ary, Mother of our Redeemer and Mother of the Church, we offer you the praise of the angel of the Annunciation – hail, full of grace! Through you the Holy Spirit gave this world Jesus its Savior – Son of God, Word made flesh, foundation of the Church.

Monday

*T*hrough you God's holy people, his Church on earth, appeals for light and strength in its pilgrimage of faith. You have gone before us on the same journey and are now glorified in heaven. Be for us who are still on that journey of faith a true Star of the Sea, leading us to the presence of your Son where he sits at the right hand of the Father, enthroned in glory.

Tuesday

*Y*ou were the first to believe. You persevered in prayer with the disciples in the Upper Room. You were a unique witness to the mystery of Jesus. All generations have called you blessed. Now God's holy Church looks yet again to you for inspiration and help.

Wednesday

*B*e our Mother. Share with us your limitless faith. Take and keep us within your protective arms in a world that has largely lost faith and abandoned hope. Petition for us from your Son – as once you did so powerfully at Cana of Galilee – an increase of vocations to the priesthood and the religious life so that the Church may flourish in our time and thereby magnify his name. Touch the hearts of all our youth that they may see in every walk of life an opportunity to serve.

Thursday

*T*ake from all our hearts the selfishness that sours relationships and keeps us centered only on ourselves. Give us hearts aflame with charity and filled with love. Make us, like the apostle John who was commended to your care, loving children of our heavenly Father, conscious always of your maternal presence in our lives.

Friday

*L*ook favorably upon your children in our failure to provide the one flock under one shepherd for which Jesus prayed. Shine forth for us and for all the peoples as a sign of sure hope and solace as we strive to make our pilgrimage of faith hand in hand. Be our common Mother who prays for the unity of God's family. May we see in you our model of that obedience of faith which should be found in all who listen attentively to what the Spirit is saying to the Churches.

Saturday

*H*e who is mighty has done great things for you. Humbly we ask that you in turn may do for us these things for which we pray in the name and through the power of that most Holy Spirit who lives and reigns in the unity of the Father and the Son, one God, forever and ever. Amen.

Prayer to Our Lady of Fatima

*M*ost Holy Virgin, who appeared at Fatima, to reveal to the three shepherds the treasures of graces hidden in the recitation of the Rosary. Inspire our hearts with a sincere love of this devotion, in order that by meditating on the Mysteries of our Redemption that are recalled in it, we may gather the fruits and obtain the conversion of sinners, and *(here name the other favors you are praying for)*, which we ask of you in this Novena, for the greater glory of God, for hour own honor, and for the good of souls. Amen.